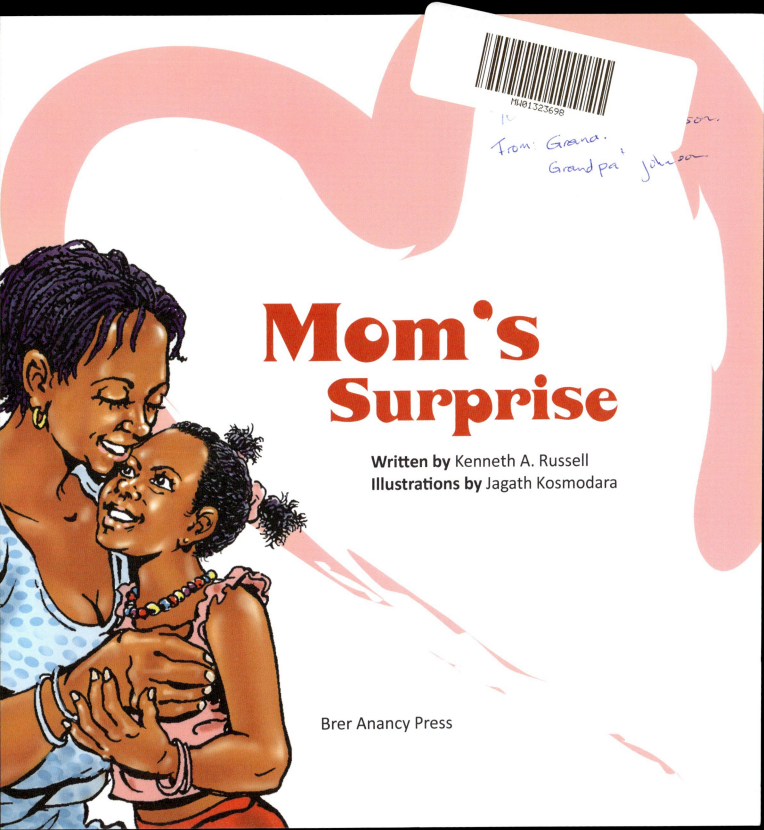

Mom's Surprise

Written by Kenneth A. Russell
Illustrations by Jagath Kosmodara

Brer Anancy Press

Mom's Surprise

All rights reserved.

Copyright © 2014 by Kenneth Russell

Cover Illustration @ 2014 Kenneth Russell.
All rights reserved – used with permission

Illustrations by Jagath Kosmodara.
All rights reserved – used with permission

This book or any portion thereof may not be reproduced or used in any manner, except for the use of brief quotations in critical articles and book reviews, without the express written permission of the publisher.

First Edition

ISBN-13: 978-1495964442

Ordering Information:

Quantity sales: Special discounts are available on quantity purchases by corporations, associations, and others.

For details contact

Bre'r Anancy Press

P.O. Box 361582

Los Angeles, CA 90036

info@breranancy.com

Printed in the United States

"BOO!" said Mommy.

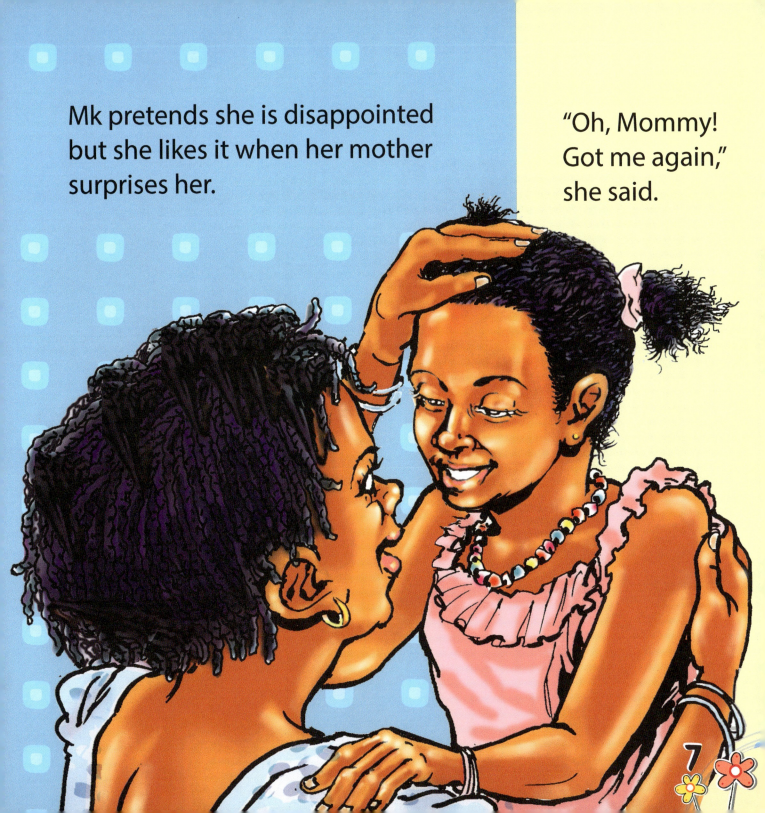

Mk pretends she is disappointed but she likes it when her mother surprises her.

"Oh, Mommy! Got me again," she said.

"Now, I have a **SURPRISE** for you," said Mk.

"I like **SURPRISES**," said Mommy. "What is it? Tell me! Tell me!" Mommy said playfully.

"You have to guess by **my actions**," said Mk. "Everything that I do will help to show you your surprise."

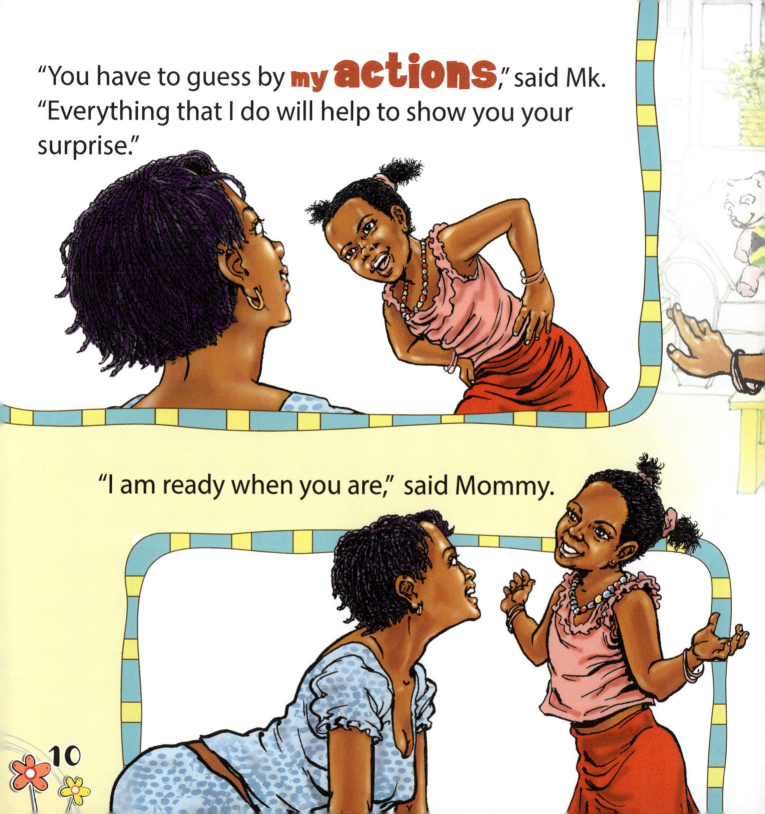

"I am ready when you are," said Mommy.

Mk JUMPED MOVED AROUND and DANCED

"I know," said Mommy, "it moves a lot."

"No, Mommy," said Mk. "Please try again."

Mk opened her arms and moved towards Mommy for a hug.

"And it is ALWAYS yours, Mommy," Mk said.

"Well, Mk," said Mommy, **"THIS** is my love for you."

"I LOVE YOU, my princess," said Mommy.

"I LOVE YOU TOO, my Mommy," said Mk.

"M-k! M-k!" called a little voice.

"Yes, Zee," said Mk, as she turned towards her little brother.

"Daddy is ready," whispered Zee.

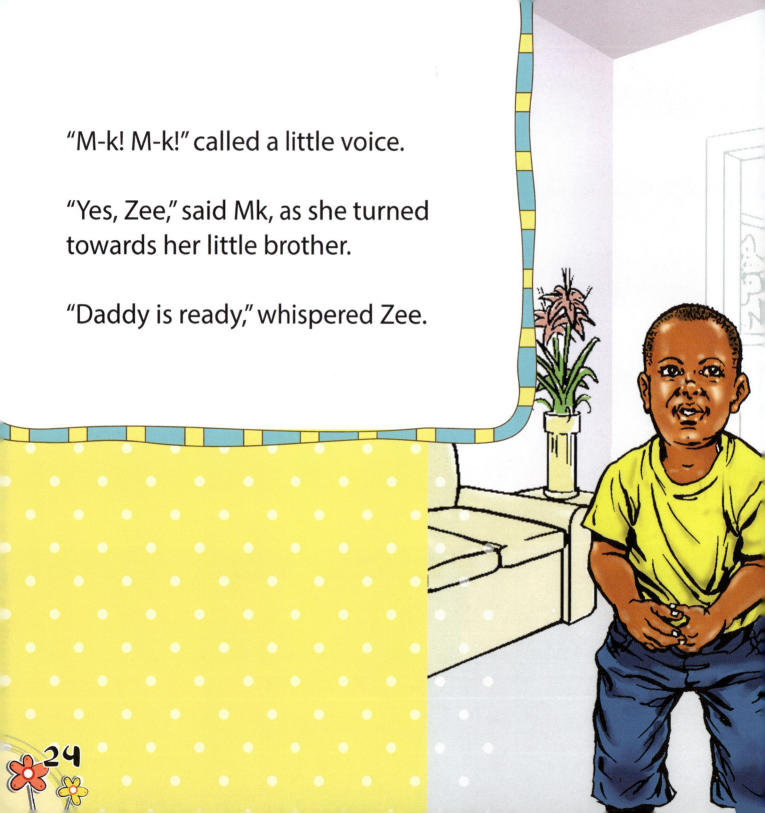

"What is Daddy doing?" Mommy asked.

"Making up your SURPRISE birthday …," Zee started to say.

His sister tried to stop him but **it was too late**.

The secret was **OUT**.

Made in the USA
Charleston, SC
22 July 2015